D0819844

No Backbone!
The World of Invertebrates

Gooey Jellyfish

by Natalie Lunis

Consultant: Bill Murphy
Marine Biologist, Northern Waters Gallery
New England Aquarium
Boston, MA

BEARPORT
PUBLISHING

NEW YORK, NEW YORK

Credits

Cover and TOC, © JJJ/Shutterstock, © Bobby Deal/RealDealPhoto/Shutterstock, © Ann Marie Hughes/Shutterstock; Title Page, © Bobby Deal/RealDealPhoto/Shutterstock; 4, © Ivan Tihelka/Shutterstock; 5, © Sissie Brimberg/National Geographic/Getty Images; 6, © Mark Conlin/V&W/imagequestmarine.com; 7, © Mike Severns/SeaPics.com; 8TL, © Norman Chan/Shutterstock; 8TR, © John Carleton/Shutterstock; 8B, © Arnold John Labrentz/Shutterstock; 9, © David B. Fleethank/SeaPics.com; 10, © David Wrobel/SeaPics.com; 11, © Phanie/Photo Researchers, Inc.; 12, © Peter Parks/Iq3-d/SeaPics.com; 13, © Ross Armstrong/SeaPics.com; 14, © Wendy Conway/Alamy; 15, © Reinhard Dirscherl/SeaPics.com; 16–17, © Paul A. Sutherland; 18, © Tim Graham/Getty Images; 19, © Roger Steene/Image Quest Marine; 21, © Norbert Wu/Minden Pictures; 22TL, © Franco Banfi/SeaPics.com; 22TR, © Marc Chamberlain/SeaPics.com; 22BL, © Mark Aplet/Shutterstock; 22BR, © David Wrobel/SeaPics.com; 22 Spot, © Sergey Popov/Shutterstock; 23TL, © Jim Wehtje/Photodisc Green/Getty Images; 23TR, © Mark Conlin/SeaPics.com; 23BL, © Peter Parks/Iq3-d/SeaPics.com; 23BR, © Scott Leslie/SeaPics.com.

Publisher: Kenn Goin
Editorial Director: Adam Siegel
Creative Director: Spencer Brinker
Design: Dawn Beard Creative
Photo Researcher: Marty Levick

Library of Congress Cataloging-in-Publication Data

Lunis, Natalie.
Gooey jellyfish / by Natalie Lunis.
   p. cm. — (No backbone! : the world of invertebrates)
Includes bibliographical references and index.
ISBN-13: 978-1-59716-510-5 (library binding)
ISBN-10: 1-59716-510-7 (library binding)
1. Jellyfishes—Juvenile literature. I. Title.

QL377.S4L86 2008
593.5'3—dc22

                              2007007986

For more information, write to Bearport Publishing Company, Inc., 101 Fifth Avenue, Suite 6R, New York, New York 10003. Printed in the United States of America.

10 9 8 7 6 5 4 3 2 1

Contents

No Bones

Jellyfish are animals that live in the sea.

They are not really fish, however.

Every kind of fish has a skeleton with a **backbone**.

backbone

Jellyfish don't have backbones.

They don't have any bones at all!

Since jellyfish are not fish, some people call them "jellies" or "sea jellies."

Bell-Shaped Bodies

Bones aren't the only thing jellyfish don't have.

They don't have brains, hearts, or blood, either.

They do have lots of jelly in their bell-shaped bodies.

They also have mouths and stomachs.

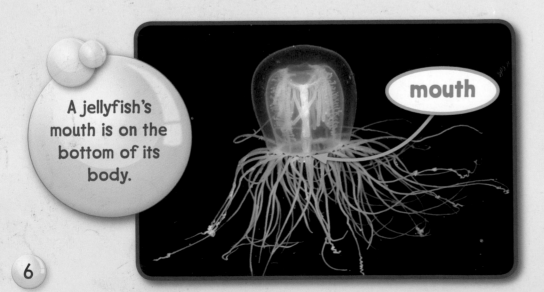

A jellyfish's mouth is on the bottom of its body.

mouth

Large and Small

There are about 2,000 kinds of jellyfish.

The largest jellyfish is larger than a person.

The smallest is smaller than a grape.

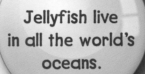
Jellyfish live in all the world's oceans.

Stinging Strands

Most jellyfish have **tentacles** and **feeding arms** hanging down from their bodies.

These body parts look like strands of seaweed.

They are not harmless, however.

They can have a deadly sting.

Some jellyfish have tentacles that are more than 100 feet (30 m) long. Others have tentacles that are almost too small to see.

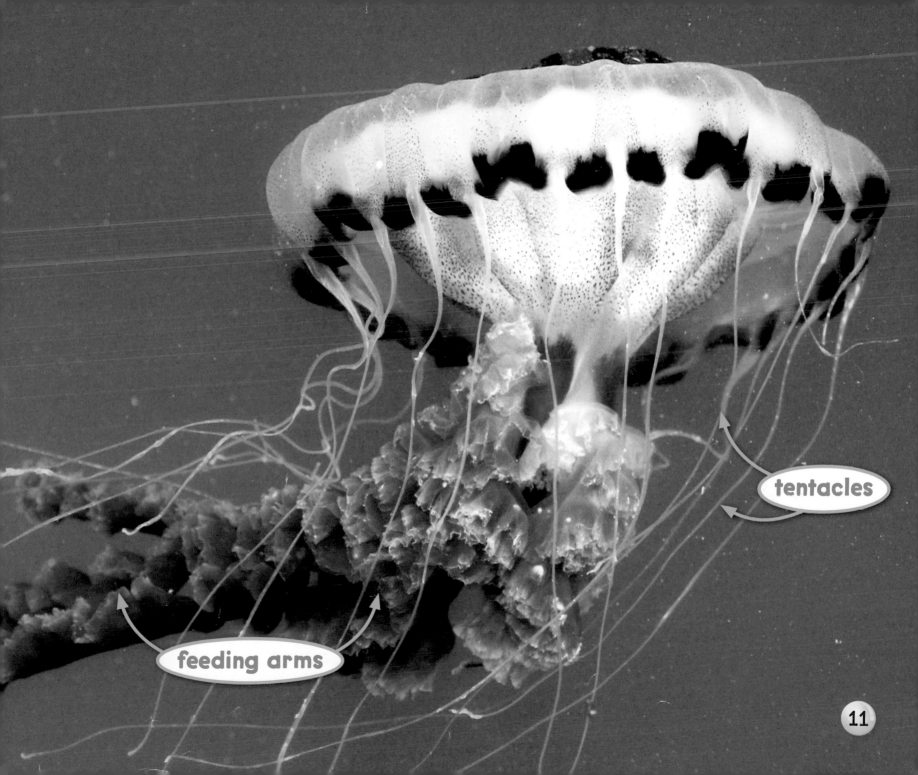

tentacles

feeding arms

Floating Traps

Jellyfish use their tentacles to get food.

Fish sometimes swim right into them.

Thousands of tiny stingers on the tentacles kill or stun the fish.

Then the jellyfish uses its feeding arms to pull the food into its mouth.

plankton

Jellyfish also catch and eat **plankton**, shrimp, crabs, and other jellyfish.

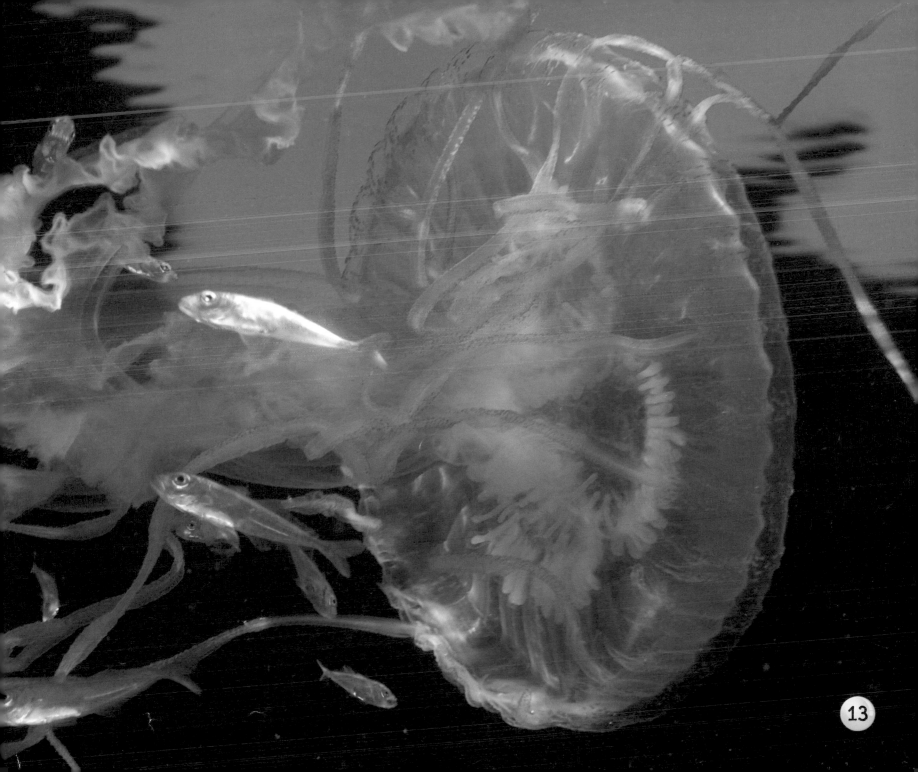

Gooey Meals

A jellyfish isn't much of a meal for other animals.

Its gooey body is mostly water.

Its tentacles can be full of poison.

Still, some fish and sea turtles hunt and eat jellyfish.

Seagulls and other birds sometimes peck at them when they wash up on shore.

jellyfish

Jellyfish are a favorite food of leatherback turtles— the largest turtles in the world.

Harmless or Harmful?

Sometimes swimmers brush against jellyfish and get stung.

The stings of most jellyfish are not harmful.

A few kinds have dangerous stings, however.

The most dangerous of all is the Australian box jellyfish.

The body of a box jellyfish is shaped like a box instead of a bell.

box jellyfish

Danger! Sea Wasp!

The Australian box jellyfish is also called the "sea wasp."

It is one of the deadliest animals on Earth.

Its sting is more poisonous than any snakebite.

Its tentacles hold enough poison to kill 60 people.

The Australian box jellyfish swims and drifts in ocean waters off Australia. Signs there warn swimmers to stay out of the water.

MARINE STINGERS ARE PRESENT IN THESE WATERS DURING THE SUMMER MONTHS

19

Floating and Fishing

No matter how poisonous they may be, jellyfish do not chase or attack people.

Instead, they spend their lives floating in the sea.

With their tentacles dangling down, they wait for their next meal to come along.

Of the 2,000 kinds of jellyfish, only about 70 can harm or kill people with their stings.

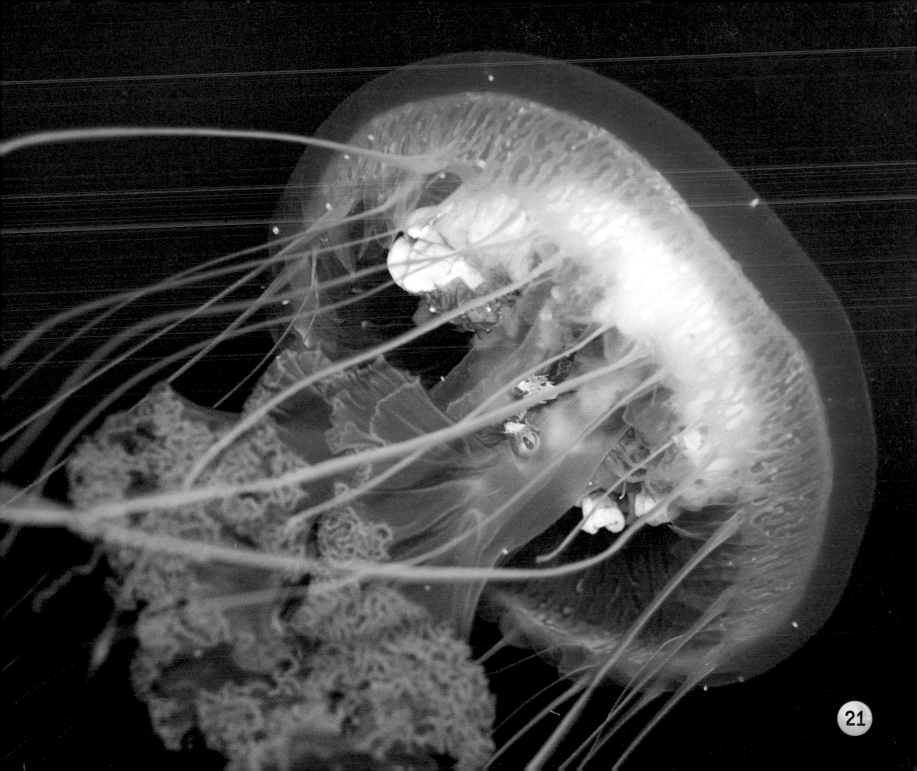

A World of Invertebrates

Animals that have backbones are known as *vertebrates* (VUR-tuh-brits). Mammals, birds, fish, reptiles, and amphibians are all vertebrates.

Animals that don't have backbones are *invertebrates* (in-VUR-tuh-brits). Worms, jellyfish, snails, and sea stars are all invertebrates. So are all insects and spiders. More than 95 percent of all kinds of animals are invertebrates.

Here are four invertebrates that are closely related to jellyfish. Like jellyfish, they all live in the ocean.

Brain Coral

Sea Pen

Sea Anemone

Comb Jelly

Glossary

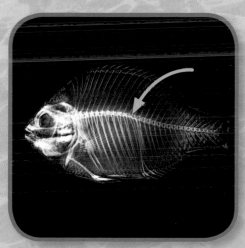

backbone
(BAK-*bohn*)
a group of connected bones that run along the backs of some animals, such as dogs, cats, and fish; also called a spine

feeding arms
(FEED-ing ARMZ)
body parts that hang down from a jellyfish's body and pull food to its mouth

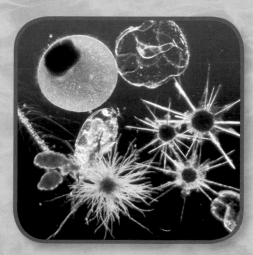

plankton
(PLANGK-tuhn)
tiny animals and plants that float in oceans and lakes

tentacles
(TEN-tuh-kuhlz)
body parts that hang down from a jellyfish's body and can sting other animals

Index

Read More

Douglas, Lloyd G. *Jellyfish.* Danbury, CT: Children's Press (2005).

Herriges, Ann. *Jellyfish (Oceans Alive).* Minneapolis, MN: Bellwether Media (2006).

Martin-James, Kathleen. *Floating Jellyfish.* Minneapolis, MN: Lerner (2001).

Learn More Online

To learn more about jellyfish, visit **www.bearportpublishing.com/NoBackbone**